User Story Confusion: Creating and Breaking Them Down

Carnsa Development Series

Chris Lewis

Published by Alderbank House, 2020.

While every precaution has been taken in the preparation of this book, the publisher assumes no responsibility for errors or omissions, or for damages resulting from the use of the information contained herein.

USER STORY CONFUSION: CREATING AND BREAKING THEM DOWN

First edition. October 20, 2020.

ISBN: 978-1393937425

Written by Chris Lewis.

Table of Contents

Dedication

To Paul, Susana, Yvonne, Harry, Jason and Katherine, a huge thank you for all your support, time and patience.

Preface

Presenting the third story in the *Carnsa Development Series called 'User Story Confusion: Creating and Breaking Them Down.'* An ideal follow-up to the Agile story called *'Agile Confusion: A Quick Understanding of the Basics and Application'.* It introduces the story-mapping technique to create user stories and options to ensure they fit into a sprint. This story is standalone, but it would be of a benefit to know the user story format, although explored in brief.

Perhaps the following scenarios are familiar to you or your team?

- We take too long to create user stories for requirements.

- As a team, we keep failing to have anything to demonstrate at the end of a sprint.

If the answer is yes to any of the above, then this book is for you!

At the end of the story, there is the usual quiz to test your knowledge.

This book may be fun, but its primary purpose is to serve as a quick and practical reference book you can refer to in the future.

The Carnsa Family

THE CARNSA FAMILY ARE a lovely, bright, and quirky family from the UK. They apply tools and techniques you may know from business and development to enhance their everyday family lives.

In each story, discover how their lives are enhanced with a tool, process, or approach. Usually, the family all get along, but occasionally, Granny, a traditionalist, will need a little more than the others to be convinced about a new approach.

Enjoy!

1. Agile Roles and User Stories

Claudia is an enthusiastic business analyst and working mother. She likes to involve her family in technology projects to learn about software and business techniques in a fun, relatable way. A persona, used in user-centred design and marketing, is a fictional person that represents a user type that might use the end service or product. It helps to understand the behaviours of a user of a service or product. A persona profile referencing Claudia could be:

- Job Role: Business Analyst Team Lead
- Lives with: Husband, four children, and her mother
- Education level: Masters
- Marital Status: Married
- Age range: 30 to 50
- Passion: Spreading good practice regarding business analysis tools and techniques
- Ability in writing using stories: 5/5 (1 = low 5 = high)

Claudia, in a user story, could be:

As a business analyst team lead, I want my team to reference the BA guidebook so that we all work in a standard way.

RECENTLY, CLAUDIA SUCCESSFULLY introduced her family to the Agile framework to help run projects. They preferred this approach over the traditional Waterfall project approach, and, as a result, they have been using it for their projects ever since. From the Agile framework, her family typically used Scrum, with time-boxed sprints of two weeks. They also used Kanban (supports continuous workflow) from the Agile framework to prepare themselves before development started. For example, the delivery of cake accessory catalogue tins and other items to help get ready before development of the cake began. The brilliant white kitchen walls took the brunt of the colourful, multiple artefact outputs created from projects. Their walls displayed various reports that included burndown charts and management dashboards to track progress. At one end was the large wooden kitchen table, where the family regularly gathered for project work.

When the family used Scrum, they ensured all the standard Agile roles represented:

- Product Owner – Representation dependent on whose project it was, had the vision, owned the requirements (user stories) backlog, and prioritised the user stories.

- Scrum Master – Typically represented by the father, Barry, who protected the team and did everything in his power to help the team focus.

- Development Team – The rest of the family, who did the actual work, selected user stories for the sprint backlog, estimated the work before the start of development, and committed to getting the work done.

• A sprint is a set time frame; for example, one to four weeks. A release contains several sprints.

The most recent project involved arranging a family holiday. In the final retrospective, the family agreed it was probably one of the best holidays they had ever had. Claudia was delighted that the family embraced and understood the user story format to capture project requirements. Evidenced by the quality of the user stories in the story map on the wall. The user story format they chose to use was:

As a **\<user type\>**, I want **\<capability\>** so that I can **\<goal\>**.

They wrote the capability section as an active verb; for example, the word 'measure' or 'read' or 'check.'

There are different ways to write a user story. For example:

• Some use the term 'I can' instead of 'I want.'

• Sometimes, the word 'capability' is replaced with the name 'feature' or 'activity.'

They understood that a user story is written from a user's point of view and that the user can be human or non-human. An example of a non-human user is a system.

An example of a user story is:

As a **driver**, I want to be **notified visually in my car when I am low on petrol** so that I can **avoid car failure**.

Note: Notified is the action verb in this example.

They adapted the approach when they tried a suggestion from Barry that worked well for them.

"At work, we write it from the user who benefits."

2. Checking Validity: INVEST

Claudia decided to check her family's knowledge of the characteristics of a good user story to check that it was valid. Otherwise, it would be most likely impractical to continue. She was in the car with her eight-year-old son, Bob.

"Bob, what is the user story format for capturing requirements?"

Bob smiled.

"It is... A **user type** wants **capability** so that I can achieve **a goal**."

She wanted to encourage Bob gently.

"Now, can you give me an example?"

There was silence for a few seconds as Bob scrunched his face.

"As a customer, I want a choice of payment methods, so I can use a method that suits me."

She grinned.

"I am very proud of you, Bob."

She decided to push him a little further.

"Do you know how we can check if a user story is ready to be developed?"

"I know! I know!" Bob could barely contain his excitement as he jiggled around in his seat.

Claudia smiled. "Go on..."

"Number one, make sure everyone is clear who the user is. Number two, make sure you write collaboratively to use the creativity and the knowledge of the team. Make certain acceptance criteria are understood by everyone, so the testing is clear."

Claudia and Bob both grinned.

"Your answer is perfect, well done. After dinner, I will show you and the family how to check if a user is valid or good."

Later after dinner, Claudia chatted about user stories.

"Now, there are lots of things you can use to help you check if a user story is good or valid. A mnemonic I use to help me remember is called '**INVEST**.' The individual letters stand for:

Independent – it stands by itself,

Negotiable – allow room for discussion,

Valuable – it is of benefit,

Estimable – the size can be estimated,

Small – the size is small and

Testable – it can be tested."

Claudia smiled as Barry, her husband, gave her a thumbs-up.

At last, something I can use to test a user story's viability, thought Barry. *I can also use this at work.*

Claudia was pleased her family were all comfortable and understood her explanation of an ideal user story.

At the table sat her ridiculously handsome husband, Barry, with his long, beautiful blond hair, and three of her four beautiful, curious children. Bob was the second-oldest child who liked using big words. The youngest of the children were Hayley and Comet, the cheeky and delightful twins. The oldest daughter, Stevie, was currently studying at university. Angela, her mother, affectionately referred to by the whole family as 'Granny,' was also at the table. She was in her eighties, a successful ex-businesswoman who came from the traditional

Waterfall style of running projects. Granny had a very close relationship with all her grandchildren. She occasionally stepped in if she felt good parenting was lacking.

3. Creating User Stories: Story Mapping

A few months ago, at the start of some of the family projects, Claudia noticed there was a difficulty when initially creating and prioritising user stories. The next time she saw their frustrated faces, she introduced the story mapping technique to create user stories. She smiled as she recalled when she first discovered the method.

"Firstly, we all need to clearly understand the vision and goal; otherwise, creating user stories will be extremely difficult."

She used the book *User Story Mapping: Building Better Products Using Agile Software Design* by Jeff Patton as a reference. Barry loved the technique and highlighted that he enjoyed the speed and visibility of it.

Today, she was almost sad as she took the story map and other project information down from the walls. Barry, still tanned from the recent holiday, came over and had a closer look at the family's handiwork on the wall. The way he stood and flicked his hair betrayed his past successful hair modelling career.

"When I brought a copy of Jeff Patton's book for work and demonstrated it, I was the hero of the week," Barry recalled as he stroked his beard.

The family used a story map to help visualise and create prioritised user stories from scratch. It showed all the user stories in context with other user stories, which gave an overall view of the project. They all worked collaboratively, and the family thought the holiday was one of the best they had ever had. She had already decided she would take a picture to go into the family project scrapbook. It was not perfect, but it was an excellent example of effective team collaboration. The story map structure had user stories along two dimensions of a horizontal and vertical axis. The horizontal axis, from left to right, told the story of the product or service. The very first row represented the highest level of user stories known as epics and was sometimes described as the walking skeleton or backbone. The epics were organised in a linear, chronological timeline as if telling the headlines of a story. The vertical axis, from top to bottom, showed decreasing priority.

Claudia had already taken down the user stories which had been captured. However, what remained on the wall was the capability part of the user story.

Barry and Claudia fondly chatted about the events that led to the family's creation of the story map. They appreciated that there were different ways to create a story map and had decided to use the following approach:

1. Identify all the possible actors.
2. Identify all the potential capabilities that formed the

capability part of the user stories.

3. Identify the capabilities in a linear, chronological order.
4. Identify related capabilities, group, and give them a label.
5. Use groupings to form and create the epics.
6. Put the capabilities under the relevant epic.
7. Rewrite the sticky capability notes as full user stories.
8. The team reviews and identifies the essential user stories.
9. The first row after the epics then forms the user stories that want to be delivered first.

The family had prepared for story mapping in the following way:

- identified a large, empty wall space in the kitchen available for the full duration of the project.

- used different colour sticky notes to represent different levels and show traceability.

- used thick marker pens to write information to read sticky notes from afar.

- used small, sticky, coloured stars to put on the sticky notes for highlighting, e.g., for prioritisation and the minimum product or service required, also known as the minimum viable product (MVP).

- used a camera to take photos of the wall.

- positioned supporting information near the relevant area of the story map for ease of relevance.

4. Disadvantages of Large User Stories

A few weeks later, at the next retrospective ceremony of the Scrum, the family highlighted a few issues they had. One of the problems was breaking down a few of the user stories to be small enough to fit into a sprint. When they came across a user story that was too big to fit into a sprint, they typically chose not to pursue it. They did this to ensure tangible items of value, so they would be able to build and demonstrate. Claudia knew if it was not immediately obvious how to refine a story, the family would skip it.

The family was presenting typical behaviour she had seen in the workplace. A large user story means a higher risk of not producing a valuable tangible item at the end of a sprint, so a team may not risk it. In Kanban, a story that is too big could end up in the equivalent of the 'in progress' column for a long time. Taking longer to get to the demonstrable tangible item might mean a delay in feedback.

When a story is too big, it becomes harder for the team to remember all the details. As a result, there is a possibility that misunderstandings and errors may occur. To counteract this, teams tend to generate a need to write down as many details as possible, which can also reduce the shared understanding. A story needs to have acceptance criteria to be considered for development. The team soon realised it was much easier to write acceptance criteria when a story is smaller and well understood.

Later, in bed, Claudia and Barry were about to reflect on the day's events. Claudia's forehead wrinkled, and then she smiled.

"I know I have to ease the family into not automatically ignoring user stories if they are too big. Understanding techniques to break down user stories will make project development so much easier."

Barry wrinkled his brow while he thought about the younger children's ability to grasp the concept.

"Don't you think the concept will be too complex for the twins to handle? They have not even started preschool level yet!"

She smiled and recalled when some of her colleagues at work were experiencing difficulties breaking down user stories. As a result, she had run a series of workshops to help highlight some of the different approaches her colleagues at work could try. Claudia knew she had to be careful with her explanation; all her children were unusually bright, but they were not child geniuses. However, she did have suspicions about her son Bob, who had recently turned eight.

"As long as they get a general idea to support the explanation, I just need to create a relatable scenario. The key thing is that the team should support each other in understanding and breaking down user stories."

The next day, after dinner, Claudia asked her family about breaking down user stories.

I have a smart family; I know they can handle this.

She took a deep breath.

"Okay, so how do we break down a complex story that is too large?"

Too late, she realised that she might have pushed them too far, as blank stares met her in response. Bob shuffled uncomfortably in his chair, the twins laid their heads on the table, and Barry just smiled weakly.

After a few seconds, Granny managed to shake herself out from her boredom trance and decided to save her family... yet again. She not-so-gently squeezed Claudia's arm and made sure she met her gaze. She leant over and whispered into Claudia's ear, "No..."

Granny turned to look at the rest of the family.

"Breaking down user stories can wait. What is more important is helping me find the right outfit for my cruise next week."

Everyone looked at Claudia to check she was okay with the suggestion. Fortunately, Claudia had got the hint and realised that she had pushed her family too far and put them into the panic zone of thinking. Claudia shrugged her shoulders and smiled.

"That sounds like a great idea! Now, what about that lovely blue and grey outfit you had custom made?"

The next day, Claudia was sitting in the hairdressers, chatting with her favourite hairdresser, Luis, about a potential haircut. He was originally from France and had come to England three years ago. He had set up a popular salon in the village. She was getting bored with her current hairstyle, despite it being easy to maintain, which was a significant plus factor for her. After inspiration from a recent film, she wanted something vastly different from her regular hairstyle. Luis and Claudia had been working together to grow her hair into a chic, one-length straight bob. Claudia trusted Luis implicitly with her hair; he always listened. However, Luis was in shock when Claudia showed him the picture of the hairstyle she wanted. The hairstyle would be a dramatic change to her usual look. Luis shook his head in dismay when he saw the picture.

"*Non*!"

Claudia raised a small smile.

"Just to be clear, I don't mind if my hair is short."

"This is not short; this is bald! *Non*! Today, we will style it differently, and you can think about it... and then next time, we will see."

Claudia raised a bigger small smile.

"Excuse me?"

Luis stood behind Claudia as he examined the condition of her hair.

"Don't worry. You tell me what you like and don't like, and we can do a small change if needed. Every time you will have something different, which is what you want? Is this not what you want? You have beautiful, thick hair; let's not do something you will regret!"

"Oh, I see. You don't want me to have a big bang change?"

Luis confirmed that this was indeed the case.

"*Oui!*"

"I guess... a change in hairstyle each time would satisfy the acceptance criteria to be different, and the final one could be the shaved version!"

At hearing the word 'shaved,' Luis took a short intake of breath.

"Okay... you may even find yourself saying 'I like this style; no more change.' If you do everything at once, you may not like such a big change."

She paused for a few seconds and tilted her head.

"Okay—let's break the process down into manageable chunks. Let's just style it differently today, and I can go for the cut next time."

He gently turned her head from him back to the mirror; he wanted to distract her so he could discreetly put the picture of the hairstyle into the bin.

Just over an hour later, she left the hairdresser with a fabulous, bouncy, curly new hairstyle. When she arrived at her friend's house later for a dinner party, compliments rained down on her about her hair. At the party, she mentioned the potential hairstyle, and at that point, she realised she no longer had the picture and smiled. Unfortunately, without the picture, and with the way Claudia described the hairstyle she originally wanted, it did not sound appealing to her friends. Her friends thought Luis was a fantastic hairdresser and he was great because he stopped Claudia from doing something drastic with her hair again.

Later that night, Claudia was talking to Barry about the day's events. They were discussing the family problem of breaking down user stories.

"It's like when you break down user stories. It is much easier if you break it down and deliver it in smaller parts rather than one big delivery."

The next day, when driving Bob back to school, Claudia thought she would take the opportunity to ask him a few questions. She was delighted with her son's grasp of user stories and decided to test him a little more.

She let silence pass for a few seconds and then decided to try another question. She felt she could push a little further.

"How would you break down your user story?"

In response, he raised his eyebrows, and his eyes widened. Claudia decided to give him a quick example to relieve the tension.

"That is a tough one, but an example could be 'As a customer, I can choose to pay by credit card' or 'As a customer, I can choose to pay by cash.' 'As a customer, I can choose to pay by bank transfer.'

Anyway, tell me what you did at school today. Cricket, wasn't it?"

They continued happily talking about Bob's school day, and the atmosphere became relaxed once more.

Bob had been upset by the breaking down story question but tried to hide it. He did not want her to know he did not understand and needed a way to find out without her knowing. Bob decided to ask his teacher, Miss Lamb, for help. He remembered his teacher had said if you could not talk to your parents, you could always talk to her.

Miss Lamb was Bob's favourite teacher and considered Bob among her brightest and most thoughtful students. She was tall, had a small button nose, and wore her hair in a high ponytail. She noticed that Bob did not join the rest of his class in the playground. Instead, he had hung back intending to talk to her.

"Miss Lamb, can I have a 'one to one' at the next playtime session, please?"

Miss Lamb thought Bob possessed intelligence beyond his years. She found him a thoughtful and kind boy. However, it was unusual for Bob to ask to talk to her.

When playtime came, Miss Lamb found Bob coming towards her, wringing his hands. She smiled, tilted her head, and invited him to sit down in the chair opposite hers. Miss Lamb encouraged Bob to speak.

"I can't talk to Mummy about something, but then I remembered you said I could talk to you if I cannot talk to my parents."

Miss Lamb smiled.

"Of course, Bob. You can ask me anything."

Bob shifted awkwardly in his chair. Miss Lamb had no idea what this was about, and her smile wavered. Miss Lamb had always thought Bob's home life was a happy one and felt a little anxious with Bob's sad demeanour. She needed to know why Bob had come to her.

"Go on. You know you can talk to me about anything."

Bob sat up in his chair, but his shoulders were still slumped and took a deep breath.

"It's about using user stories in the family project. I don't want to tell Mummy that I don't know how to break down user stories to fit in a sprint."

Miss Lamb looked at Bob in surprise and disbelief.

"Yes, Miss Lamb. I know it's bad."

Unfortunately, this was a subject Miss Lamb hadn't expected to be asked about and realised the stack of support leaflets that she had in readiness were useless. The leaflets covered subjects to deal with bullying, acne, and bereavement.

Crikey, thought Miss Lamb, *I have no idea what Agile is, let alone what a user story is.*

Miss Lamb wished she had a guide to just get the Agile basics. She was now concerned by how upset Bob was and wanted to find a practical way to help him.

"Is there someone else in your family you can ask who could help you?"

Bob's face brightened as he realised there was someone he could ask.

"I could ask Granny! She is very old, so she knows lots of stuff. I could ask her to tell me. That would be a good plan."

Miss Lamb was hugely relieved, as it avoided the need to deal with the computer teacher to try and find an answer for Bob.

Later that day, Bob was alone with Granny.

"I don't want to let Mummy down."

Granny reached out to Bob and gave him a big hug, puzzled at his sudden outburst.

"Now tell me: what on Earth is the matter?"

"How can I make sure a user story is small enough to fit into a sprint? Can you help me find out without letting Mummy know I am asking? I don't want Mummy to think I am not a clever boy."

Granny was relieved but also annoyed at the distress and confusion her daughter had caused her grandchildren yet again. She believed young children's biggest dilemmas in life should be about when the next packet of sweets would appear or when they would see their friends.

"You are the cleverest eight-year-old boy I know! Your mummy will never stop thinking you are a clever boy, and we all need to learn sometime."

Granny highlighted to Bob that she also did not understand how to break down larger user stories either. However, she would talk to Claudia but be discreet and not let her know the source of her enquiry. Granny took both of Bob's hands, held them gently, and then gave them a brief squeeze. Granny then tilted her head and looked him in the eyes.

"Leave it to me. I will sort something out for you by bedtime."

Granny immediately went to look for Claudia and eventually found her in the oak-panelled study.

"Claudia, explain to me briefly some ways to break down user stories to fit into a sprint."

Claudia coughed and spluttered, spitting her tea out everywhere. She wished someone else could hear Granny ask her for help. Granny kept her promise to Bob and did not tell Claudia the real reason she was interested.

"Claudia, before you start, talk me through an example first and then tell me the benefits."

Granny wanted to ensure that there was a clear structure that she could follow, as Claudia explained.

"Okay, remember when we did the project for Barry's birthday?"

5. A Tangible User Story Every Sprint

Claudia recalled the project when Barry wanted a pirate-themed vanilla birthday cake; they had used the Scrum framework for project development. She was delighted that the family was able to produce, at the end of every sprint, a tangible demonstrable item of value. Barry represented the product owner, and Granny represented the Scrum master. The first sprint produced a plain vanilla cupcake and a pirate flag iced on top.

At the end of the first sprint show and tell demonstration, Barry changed his requirement and decided he wanted chocolate cake. The change was not a problem for the family development team because they were prepared for the possibility of changes as a result of feedback. Feedback at such an early stage made it easy to change.

In the Scrum planning ceremony, the family selected the next sprint items from the main backlog for their sprint backlog. They selected accordingly based on the feedback and prioritisation information they had. In the second sprint, the team produced a chocolate cake in the shape of a pirate boat. The third sprint consisted of a pirate boat-shaped cake with a flag and edible pirate figures inside the boat. Granny was particularly pleased with the decoration and rated it among her best designs. Barry was so impressed with the demonstration at the third sprint that he was happy to accept the work as it was. The family team was surprised but delighted that they did not have to do any more work, and there was a leftover budget. He liked the way he could see a tangible item every sprint and stop unnecessary work when happy with the result.

"I liked the fact I had a chance to see what was going on and give feedback at regular intervals. A key point for me as the business was to get on board and understand the big picture."

6. Benefits of Breaking Down User Stories

After about an hour, Granny reckoned she had all the main points but wasn't a hundred percent sure. Granny impatiently tapped her notebook.

"Okay, I now understand the value of breaking down sprints into tangible items of value every time, but what about the other benefits?"

She pushed her notebook forward on the pages to be read by Claudia.

"Just tell me if anything captured in my notes is wrong."

Claudia picked up the notebook, pushed her glasses up her nose, and leant forward to read them more closely. The handwriting was neat and precise. She read:

Benefits

- Faster feedback loops.

- Progress every day.

- Small wins every day.

- Happier team.

- Greater engagement with the business.

- Improves shared understanding.

- Increases the accuracy of estimation.

- Supports the product owner in the prioritisation of work.

- Developers do not need to coordinate between different layers.

- The customer sees the results of each story, which means the developers can get constant input from the customer.

After a few minutes, when Claudia finished, Granny asked: "Have I missed anything?"

Claudia reread the notes.

"No, your notes are spot on!"

Wow! She has been listening to me. I can build on this.

"Now, let me recap some of the different ways you can break down user stories."

Granny let out a deep sigh and started to shake her head.

"No, don't do that. Just look at my notes and tell me if anything is wrong about breaking down user stories."

Claudia leaned forward to read the notes:

- **Is everything needed?**

- Could you remove the 'nice to have' until you get confirmation that they are required?

- **Is it a complicated interface?**

- Can you create a simple one first?

• Is the story affected by multiple business rules?

- Try a subset of rules first.
- Example/notes:

▪ As a shop owner, I can add free delivery for orders above £30.

▪ As a shop owner, I can cancel orders for a payment not received within 48 hours.

• Does the story describe a workflow?

- Try starting with just the start and end stages and then add the middle bits later.

• Is the story more complicated because of the non-functional requirements (NFR)?

- Try to satisfy the non-NFR bit first.
- Example/notes:

▪ As a shopper, I receive a container so that I can carry items I will purchase.

▪ As a shopper, I receive a bag so that I can hold at least 10 kg, so I can carry items I am interested in.

• Can the story be broken down into workflow steps?

- Try each step as a separate story.

• Does the story do the same process for different types of data?

- Try processing one piece of data first and add or enhance the others later.
- The first story could have most effort upfront, and then the others that are similar to it will be smaller.
- Example/notes:

▪ Accepting different types of credit cards, could you start with one type first?

• Does the story have multiple interfaces?

- Try a simple one first.

• Is there a central/core piece to the story?

- Try doing the core first.

• Does the story include multiple operations?

- Try splitting the story into separate operations.

• Absolutely no idea after trying all the other tips?

- Is there a small bit you can understand?
- Can you identify critical questions holding you back?

Claudia grinned.

"All correct, you have summarised it very well. Now, let me go into some detail of…"

Granny immediately put two fingers close together up to her lips, which signalled Claudia to stop talking, and she started to walk out.

"No need for more chat. I have everything I need. Thank you, I have to go."

Claudia mumbled under her breath, *"Acceptance criteria is key to the creation of a valid user story; it is incomplete without it…. You don't understand what good looks like."*

Granny walked into the living room and started to write more notes to find a quick and easy way she could explain breaking down user stories. Eventually, she came up with an idea to create a bedtime story.

Barry was curious about what Granny was up to when he found her in the living room with a large amount of paper crumpled and discarded in the bin. She looked up and saw him and decided to put her plan into action straight away.

"I will be covering the bedtime story shift this evening with Bob."

"No, it's okay, I have already planned a story about robots and knights. It is very cool, and he will love it. Why don't you do it tomorrow night instead?"

Granny appreciated the effort he had put in. She held her hands in his and proceeded to tell him about her breaking down user story conversation with Bob. She also highlighted she was concerned that Bob dwelled on things that should not be the concern of such a young child. He hung his head guiltily in response.

"I am glad Bob feels comfortable talking to you, thank you."
They hugged.

"He comes to you and Claudia for the things that matter, and that is what counts."

He smiled a little and shrugged his shoulders.

"I guess so... Hey, let's create the bedtime story together. I have a few ideas to help Bob with his understanding, and we can include some elements I know he will like."

"Now that sounds like a jolly good idea. Let's crack on," said Granny.

Granny and Barry created a bedtime story to ensure the goal of the requirement was clear. They naturally created a user story as a starting point of reference. Claudia would have been pleased. The user story they created was:

As a team member, I want to be aware of different approaches so that I can use it to help break down user stories to fit into a sprint.

They then broke down the user story to:

As a team member, I want a mnemonic that can help me think of breakdown user story options so that I can help the team fit a user story into a sprint.

As a team member, I want a quick way that can help me think of breakdown user story options so that I can help the team fit a user story into a sprint.

A couple of hours later, they looked at their story captured on pages of notes now stacked on the coffee table in front of them. They simultaneously fist bumped in the air.

Later, at dinner, Granny announced she would cover Storytime for Bob that night. She then winked at Bob.

"I have an extraordinary story for you."

Later, when it was time for Bob's bedtime. Barry and Claudia discreetly listened outside Bob's bedroom. Claudia had learnt about Granny's plan from Barry, and she was enormously grateful.

7. A Bedtime Story

When the time for Bob's bedtime story came, Granny knocked on his door.

"Bob, are you ready for an extra special story?"

He stopped what he was doing and dived into bed.

"Yes, yes, come in!"

Bob's bedroom had posters of planets and robots. Towards the back was a large table with a chemistry set, train tracks, and trains. She came into Bob's room and tucked the covers all around him, so only his head peeped out. Just the way he liked it. She then sat on the comfortable armchair next to the bed. She got herself comfortable in the big, dark blue chair with lemon-coloured cushions.

"Are you ready for me to start the story?"

"Yes, please!"

Bob closed his eyes in anticipation.

"Then, I will start."

Granny held in her hand a stapled stack of paper, which was titled *Bob's Story*. She put her reading glassed on, adjusted her position in the chair, and read from her notes.

"There is a distant planet called Bob, which is like Earth, but three hundred years ahead in technology innovation. On the planet lived a little boy named Denzel, who was eight years old and had two multicoloured robotic pets, a robotic ram, and a robotic cow. Denzel's parents liked him to have plenty of exercise and fresh air. As a result, they bought him the pets to encourage him to exercise. Denzel named his multicolour pets Rob and Bert. He loved his pets, and not just because he did not have to clear up any poo like some of his other friends who had real pets. His pets registered the amount of daily exercise Denzel undertook and then sent a report back to his parents. Denzel was close to his Granny and visited her often.

"Granny had warned Denzel that she would be having visitors, her next-door neighbours, Mr and Miss Smith, the day Denzel was visiting. They were big cake eaters, like Denzel. Mr and Miss Smith just needed to nip through the garden hedge to knock on Granny's door, and typically arrived at three-thirty in the afternoon for a chat and to drink tea and eat cake. They were always on time. Granny tells Denzel that if he can get to her before three fifteen in the afternoon, she would be able to guarantee him a slice of cake. Afterwards, it would be unlikely that there would be any left. Denzel usually left home at two forty-five in the afternoon after completion of his chores. Granny lived on the other side of a small stream with a small bridge deliberately kept narrow to discourage cars. The entrance to Granny's house was along a path with a tall, narrow gate at the end. Denzel was very excited by Granny's news because he did not get much cake at home. His parents' idea of a treat was typically carrot sticks with hummus. It was just one of the many reasons why he loved to visit Granny. Sometimes, he just wanted something sweet.

"Denzel knew, the quicker he could get his pets through the gate, the faster his chance of a slice of cake. He tried to leave his pets at home, so he did not have to tend to them on his way to Granny. Unfortunately, his parents would not let him leave his pets behind.

"The first time Denzel visited his Granny, both his pets, Rob and Bert, got stuck in the gate at the same time in front of him, but by the time he managed to free them, he was too late for cake. Denzel was not one to give up. The second time, Denzel encouraged Rob the ram to go through the gate first because it was faster, leaving the slow Bert the cow behind. However, by the time Denzel had helped Bert the cow through, he was too late for cake. After the visit, Denzel had an idea for next time. He asked his parents if he could take just one pet. Still, his parents explained he must take both for the exercise tracking software to work correctly. Denzel tried to sort out the cake-visiting dilemma with his Granny.

'Wait a minute. Don't you have the pet version five-eight-seven series?'

'Yes.'

'That version allows you to break the larger pets into a completely different colour and smaller versions of themselves.
'

"Denzel punched his fist in the air with joy.

'That is terrific news.
'

"He checked with his parents, and they approved the smaller versions when he showed them because they were complete.

"The next Saturday, Denzel reduced his pets down into nine small, complete versions of themselves and popped four of them, the blue versions, into his shirt pocket, and ran with them to Granny's house. He managed to get to Granny's at twelve minutes past three and ate a slice of cake with Granny and her friends.

"The end!"

8. Breaking Down Tips

Bob could not help but smile from ear to ear when Granny finished his unique bedtime story.

"That was fantastic. Thank you."

Granny smiled.

"So, tell me, what did you learn from the story about user stories?"

He paused and tilted his head.

"Not to give up when a user story is too big. Broken down stories must still be able to be used to provide complete tangible items. Ummm... not everything needs to be included as long as it can be considered complete in each sprint."

"Well done, that is exactly right."

Granny spotted Barry outside and beckoned him in. Claudia had already crept away, as she did not want Bob to see her.

Barry spoke up. "I think I have something to help you remember some different options you can try out when breaking down user stories. Are you interested?"

"Yes, please."

He had created a mnemonic, and it was BI COW RAM, which stood for:

- Business rules
- Interface
- Core
- Operations

- Workflow
- Research
- All Processes
- Must Haves

· He had created a mnemonic, and it was BI COW RAM.

An example of BICOWRAM in the use of using bank services via an ATM machine could be:

· **B**usiness rules – can you select one or a few related rules, E.g. in a cash machine scenario, only users who enter the correct pin can access bank services.

· **I**nterface – is there a more straightforward version you can use? E.g. use a simpler interface with choices drilled down as needed.

· **C**ore – identify key areas to be addressed? E.g. withdrawing cash.

· **O**perations – can this be broken down? E.g. identify the process of pin entry, confirm pin, start a transaction, end transaction.

· **W**orkflow – can you be selective? E.g. look at the process, can you identify the trigger, endpoint and select a particular process, e.g. viewing a balance.

· **R**esearch – are there areas you want to know more about, that you want to explore? E.g. linking to mobile services.

· **A**ll processes – can you select a category? E.g. processes that relate to viewing balances.

· **M**ust haves – check identified by the customer and not just an assumption by you? E.g. clarify who sourced the user story and their motivation.

Bob gently smiled, and his shoulders relaxed. He finally understood how he could break down user stories that were too big to fit into a sprint.

"Thank you so much."

Bob suddenly sat up, bolt upright, remembering his training from Claudia when analysing and understanding options.

"I need an example I can relate to, please."

Barry smiled.

"Absolutely. If you remember, a user story that was not used in the backlog was family camping with a music festival. We could have broken that story down to two complete smaller user stories. The user stories evolved around camping in the garden, getting pizza delivery, watching festival music on the big television, or going to a festival with a range of music booked with appropriate accommodation."

Bob laughed.

"That is silly, but I know what you mean. Yes, thank you!"

Granny's shoulders started to bunch up. She took a few deep breaths.

"Now, here is a less silly example. Exploring a user story may reveal multiple business rules, which may be a good story on its own. For example, if you had the user story:

As a user, I can search for package holidays with flexible dates. You could break it down to:

As a user, I can search for a package holiday with different day lengths between 1 and 30.

As a user, I can search for availability in a particular month.

As a user, I can search for weekends in a particular month."

Bob glanced at his father and smiled.

"Thank you, Granny. They are great examples."

The next day, Bob and his mother Claudia were in the car on the way to school.

"How are you feeling today, Bob?"

Bob smiled.

"BI... COW... RAM!"

Claudia smiled.

"Pardon?"

"I am using a mnemonic, which is a pattern of letters, ideas, or associations that helps in remembering something. I am saying BI then COW then RAM. Think of bionic animals, a ram and a cow."

Bob then proceeded to explain what the letters in BICOWRAM stood for.

As they walked to the school gates, she stopped and gave Bob a big hug and ruffled his hair.

"I am very impressed with you, Bob. I am going to tell my friends at work about the mnemonic. Do you know, it took me a while to fully understand options I could consider for breaking down user stories? You are the cleverest eight-year-old boy I know, not just because you know a lot but because you are not afraid to ask questions."

Claudia took Bob's hands and held them gently in hers and smiled.

"You know, Bob, it is very powerful to say you don't know and to ask for help. Please never be worried about saying, 'I don't know.'"

Bob grinned.

"Mummy, I am okay."

Bob hugged her and ran through the school gates. When she saw Bob, Miss Lamb asked for a quick 'one to one' before class started.

"Did you get a chance to chat with your Granny?"

He grinned from ear to ear.

"Yes, and it is all good."

He then told her all about BICOWRAM and the power of saying 'I don't know' and asking questions.

Miss Lamb relaxed in her seat and smiled.

"I am glad you are okay, and I have also learnt something as well!"

Miss Lamb realised she wanted to find some more information about Agile. She planned to do some research and see if there was a short technology reference book series to learn the basics of Agile quickly.

9. Splitting User Stories: Slicing

Claudia wanted to highlight another technique for breaking down user stories, known as 'vertical slicing' or 'horizontal slicing.' She had the perfect opportunity at family afternoon tea.

"In Agile, the objective is to have tangible items at the end of a sprint. A tangible item should be demonstratable."

Bob replied slowly.

"Yes..."

"Well, would you like to know some other ways to approach breaking down the user story and... have some cake?"

Bob smiled and grinned at the mention of cake.

"Yes."

"Bob, bring the cake to me and a knife, please."

Bob did as she asked.

"Now, cut me a slice, please."

Just before Bob started to cut the cake, Claudia put her hand on the hand Bob was about to cut the cake with.

"Stop!"

"Why?"

"Imagine you never tried this cake before. What is the best way to cut it?"

"Straight down!"

Granny could not understand all the current nonsense and drama.

"He was just doing that."

"Yes, you did it vertically. Now, here is the question. Why didn't you cut along the cake horizontally?"

Granny hunched her shoulders, and her breathing got a little faster.

"Because it would be silly." Bob began to understand what she was trying to do. "You don't know if you like it unless you try all the good bits in one go."

"Exactly, now, let me summarise. You need to try all the layers before you know if you like it. A horizontal slice would not work out because the business would not have enough information to make a judgement if they like it. Sometimes, teams in a sprint break down user stories in a horizontal layer, which is not ideal. To support business understanding and better feedback, slicing a user story vertically is recommended. A small item with all the information provided in one go is much better than delivering nothing."

"Can I have a business example, please?" said Barry as he was writing notes.

"Okay, imagine you are creating a website where people can buy flowers. In the horizontal approach, perhaps, different sprints are dedicated to different functionality. For example, the database, then the front end, and then the integration. The business can't have a go until all the layers are complete," said Claudia.

"In the vertical approach, perhaps, just the functionality of searching for flowers is done in the first sprint. Perhaps only build the elements needed for it, across all the disciplines, e.g. the database, interface, and the appropriate integration—a small section, but a section that can be demonstrated. In the next sprint, perhaps, the focus is on a search that can include optional video. At every sprint, the business can see a demonstration of a tangible item."

Granny sighed.

"Got it! I now would like to enjoy the rest of my tea and cake without a lesson, please."

The end.

10. Summary

This section is a summary of the key learning points, with some guidance and further references to explore. Sources are provided in good faith, and the inclusion of any links does not necessarily imply a recommendation or endorse the views expressed within them. Please be aware that some of these links may no longer be valid, as time may have passed by the time you read this book. Remember, these examples are not exhaustive but should give you a start in breaking down your user stories.

Approach

- Check whether the user story is valid before attempting to break it down.

- Don't give up. If at first, the user story looks unlikely to break down; consider alternative methods.

- When broken down, check if the user story is still valid.

INVEST is a mnemonic to help remember user stories. Bill Wake created the INVEST model. The individual letters stand for **I**ndependent – it stands by itself, **N**egotiable – allow room for discussion, **V**aluable – it is of benefit, **E**stimable – the size can be estimated, **S**mall – the size is small, and **T**estable – it can be tested. Remember, when breaking down user stories, the outcome needs to be a complete story (a tangible service/

delivery). The small aspect highlights the need to split large stories into smaller ones, which must still comply with the INVEST model.

A way to remember different things you can go through when faced with a large user story:

- **B**usiness Rules
- **I**nterface
- **C**ore area
- **O**perations
- **W**orkflow
- **R**esearch
- **A**ll processes
- **M**ust haves

Links

10 Useful Strategies for Breaking Down Large User Stories (and a cheat sheet) by Christiaan Verwijs

https://medium.com/the-liberators/
10-powerful-strategies-for-breaking-down-user-stories-in-scrum-w

New Story Splitting Resource January 27, 2012, by Richard Lawrence[1] from Agile for All

https://agileforall.com/new-story-splitting-resource/

Story splitting cheat sheet

https://agileforall.com/wp-content/uploads/2009/10/
Story-Splitting-Cheat-Sheet.pdf

New Story Splitting Resource January 27, 2012, | by Richard Lawrence[2] from Agile for All

https://agileforall.com/new-story-splitting-resource/

Patterns for Splitting User Stories by Richard Lawrence

---

1.   https://agileforall.com/author/rlawrence/

2.   https://agileforall.com/author/rlawrence/

https://agileforall.com/patterns-for-splitting-user-stories/

Books

User Story Mapping: Discover the Whole Story, Build the Right Product by Jeff Patton

11. Quiz

The following quiz is an opportunity to test your breaking down story knowledge and key moments from the story. Be aware that there may be occasions when there may be more than one correct answer!

1. What are not roles in the Scrum framework?

   a. Product Owner
   b. Product Manager
   c. Team Leader

2. Which frameworks from Agile does the family use to develop projects?

   a. Kanban
   b. Less
   c. Scrum
   d. SAFe

3. When should you break down a user story?

   a. When it is too big to fit into a sprint
   b. When the project manager says

4. What are the symptoms of a story that is too big in Kanban?

a. It does not progress and gets stuck for a long time
b. There is no symptom – this is a trick question!

5. What are the advantages to a team in breaking down user stories to fit into a sprint?

a. High morale
b. Easier to get feedback from the business
c. A smaller deliverable is easier to change

6. What is INVEST?

a. A way to check the validity of user stories
b. A process to break down user stories

7. What does Granny feel is more important than breaking down user stories?

a. Choosing cruise outfits
b. Delivering in the final sprint
c. SCRUM

8. What does INVEST stand for?

a. Independent, negotiable, valuable, estimable, small, and testable
b. Independent, noted, valuable, estimable, small, and testable
c. Independent, negotiable, valuable, estimable, sizeable, and testable

9. What hairstyle did Claudia's hairdresser refuse to do?

   a. Shave her hair
   b. Dye her hair blond
   c. Permanently curl her hair

10. What does the M in BICOWRAM mnemonic stand for?

   a. Must haves
   b. Mandatory
   c. Major

11. Which user story slicing approach is recommended?

   a. Vertical
   b. Diagonal
   c. Horizontal

12. What is the difficulty about using vertical slicing?

   a. It is not natural
   b. It takes practice
   c. Trick question – there are no difficulties

13. Which items are referenced in a user story format?

   a. User type
   b. Priority
   c. Capability

14. Which story mapping technique author reference does the family follow?

    a. Jeff Patton
    b. Tony Patterson
    c. Patrick Fenton

15. What does a release contain?

    a. Team organisational documents
    b. Sprints

16. What role does Barry typically play in Agile projects?

    a. Scrum master
    b. Product owner
    c. Team lead

17. What are the names of Granny's neighbours in the bedtime story?

    a. Mr & Miss Jones
    b. Mr & Miss Grey
    c. Mr & Miss Smith

18. What was the topic of the last family Agile project?

    a. A new car
    b. A family holiday
    c. Bob's birthday party

19. What should be delivered at the end of every sprint?

    a. Anything
    b. An item of tangible value
    c. The history of the work involved

20. What is/are the key advantage(s) of using a story map?

    a. Visual representation of user story in context with other stories
    b. Ideally created as a team
    c. There are not any!

21. If a user story is broken down, should it still comply with the INVEST or another model?

    a. Yes
    b. No

12. Quiz answers

This section contains the answers to the quiz from the previous section.

1. What are not roles in the Scrum framework?

✓ (a) Product Owner

2. Which frameworks from Agile does the family use to develop projects?

✓ (a) Kanban
✓ (c) Scrum

3. When should you break down a user story?

✓ (a) When it is too big to fit into a sprint

4. What are the symptoms of a story that is too big in Kanban?

✓ (a) It does not progress and gets stuck for a long time

5. What are the advantages to a team in breaking down user stories to fit into a sprint?

✓ (a) High morale
✓ (b) Easier to get feedback from the business

✓ (c) A smaller deliverable is easier to change

6. What is INVEST?

✓ (a) A way to check the validity of user stories

7. What does Granny feel is more important than breaking down user stories?

✓ (a) Choosing cruise outfits

8. What does INVEST stand for?

✓ (a) Independent, negotiable, valuable, estimable, small, and testable

9. What hairstyle did Claudia's hairdresser refuse to do?

✓ (a) Shave her hair

10. What does the M in BICOWRAM mnemonic stand for?

✓ (a) Must haves

11. Which user story slicing approach is recommended?

✓ (a) Vertical

12. What is the difficulty about using vertical slicing?

✓ (a) It is not natural
✓ (b) It takes practice

13. Which items are referenced in a user story format?

✓ (a) User type
✓ (c) Capability

14. Which story mapping technique author reference does the family follow?

✓ (a) Jeff Patton

15. What does a release contain?

✓ (b) Sprints

16. What roles does Barry typically play in Agile projects?

✓ (b) Product owner

17. What are the names of Granny's neighbours in the bedtime story?

✓ (c) Mr & Miss Smith

18. What was the topic of the last family Agile project?

✓ (b) A family holiday

19. What should be delivered at the end of every sprint?

✓ (b) An item of tangible value

20. What is/are the key advantage(s) of using a story map?

✓ (a) Visual representation of user story in context with other stories

✓ (b) Ideally created as a team

21. If a user story is broken down, should it still comply with the INVEST or another model?

✓ (a) Yes

Also by Chris Lewis

Angela Adisa
Angela Adisa. Origin: Undefined by Age Colour or Gender.
Angela Adisa. Troubled Waters: Retired Scientist. Loving
Grandmother. Secret Agent.

Carnsa Development Series
Model Confusion: The Use of Models to Support Analysis in
Projects
Agile Confusion: A Quick Understanding of the Basics and
Application
User Story Confusion: Creating and Breaking Them Down
BDD Confusion: Using Behaviour driven development for
acceptance criteria
Kanban Confusion: An Introduction to Context and Use
Change Confusion: Prepare, Support and Maintain

Jax and Sheba
Jax and Sheba get Messy

Standalone

Haley y Comet apprenden sobre el COVID-19

Haley and Comet Learn About COVID-19

Haley and Comet Learn to Plan with Kanban!

Haley dan Comet Pelajari Tentang COVID-19

Haley e Cometa aprendem sobre a COVID-19

Haley and Comet Stay at Home

Watch for more at https://www.booksbychrislewis.com/.

About the Author

Chris Lewis has a passion for learning, sharing and sometimes challenging the status quo. An author of both fiction and non-fiction books to help spread knowledge and a little fun. The Carnsa Development Series books are ideal for those who learn best from examples. They are business and technology guide books designed for reading in about an hour.

Read more at https://www.booksbychrislewis.com/.

Lightning Source UK Ltd.
Milton Keynes UK
UKHW020639110722
405680UK00010B/866